THE CHAIR

by

James A. Campbell

Road Trip Photography by

Vernon J. LaBau

Mechanicsburg, Pennsylvania   USA

Published by Sunbury Press, Inc.
50 West Main Street, Suite A
Mechanicsburg, Pennsylvania 17055

www.sunburypress.com

Copyright © 2014 by James A. Campbell.
Cover copyright © 2014 by Sunbury Press, Inc.

Sunbury Press supports copyright. Copyright fuels creativity, encourages diverse voices, promotes free speech, and creates a vibrant culture. Thank you for buying an authorized edition of this book and for complying with copyright laws by not reproducing, scanning, or distributing any part of it in any form without permission. You are supporting writers and allowing Sunbury Press to continue to publish books for every reader. For information contact Sunbury Press, Inc., Subsidiary Rights Dept., 50-A W. Main St., Mechanicsburg, PA 17011 USA or legal@sunburypress.com.

For information about special discounts for bulk purchases, please contact Sunbury Press Orders Dept. at (855) 338-8359 or orders@sunburypress.com.

To request one of our authors for speaking engagements or book signings, please contact Sunbury Press Publicity Dept. at publicity@sunburypress.com.

ISBN: 978-1-62006-495-5 (Trade Paperback)
ISBN: 978-1-62006-496-2 (Mobipocket)
ISBN: 978-1-62006-497-9 (ePub)

FIRST SUNBURY PRESS EDITION: October 2014

Product of the United States of America
0 1 1 2 3 5 8 13 21 34 55

Set in Bookman Old Style
Designed by Lawrence Knorr
Cover by Amber Rendon
Edited by Amanda Shrawder
Front cover photo courtesy of Allan C. Campbell, M.D.

Continue the Enlightenment!

This book

is dedicated to all who through the years

gave me the gift

of being their pastor.

ACKNOWLEGMENTS

Vernon J. "Jim" LaBau was crucial to the road trip with the old oak chair. The value of his photography to this book and his eye for the moment cannot be emphasized enough. Of significance was his patience in his willingness to travel with only a general direction and turn down any road on a whim. Above all is my appreciation that through the years Jim defined for me the meaning of the word "friend."

I extend my gratitude to Nancy Gresham, whose proofreading continually gave clarity to the book and whose encouragement was sustaining as each chapter found greater direction and voice. Proofreading began as an anticipated minor task but became consuming as each chapter and some sentences required more and more time. Thank you.

Thanks also to Susan Holway, among others, whose continued review of the text is most appreciated.

Finally, I give my appreciation to John and Jeani Brandt, who for a year kept the old oak chair in safekeeping before providing the chair its final journey home and also supplying photos of that trip.

INTRODUCTION

"So, what are you writing about?"
"I'm writing a book about my life with my chair."
"...oh."

This book is, in fact, about an evolving relationship to a chair. It is more than that. This book is about knowing. It is a book about discovering catalysts that can enable us to expand from awareness to the comic, to the beautiful. It is a knowing that fleshes out the spiritual mandate for justice and empathy, to live for what is healing, joyous, and redemptive. Perhaps one may call it catalytic knowing, the poetics of stone soup.

It may be that the future belongs to those who are given to multiple ways of knowing, multiple ways of discovery, play and assimilation. To such an end is the offering of this book.

CHAPTER 1
The Chair

A life by that one thing.

How many funerals through the years were planned around that thought? Show me something that is your father, his spirit, distilled into that one thing: a coffee cup, a favorite chair, a fishing rod, a photograph.

Life in that one thing.

For me, that one thing is the old oak chair and that one thing is this story. I wish I had one picture, just one, of when it all began. I doubt the chair, a captain's chair, would be the center of any photo. Most likely the chair would be in the picture's corner, out of focus, perhaps cut off in partial disclosure. Still, hopefully, there would be enough of the chair in the photo to witness to its original humbled condition and its overlooked place in the backyard. Overlooked is a good word for forgotten. That is what the old chair was, forgotten in plain sight, overlooked. Its once caned seat was missing the caning and the seat was now a piece of makeshift plywood. Its weathered layers of green, beige, orange, and turquoise paint were peeling like diseased skin.

In fairness, the chair had some utility. The family cat claimed it as a lounge. By knotting the garden hose around its arm, the chair could be posed to point the hose nozzle across the lawn or garden. Looking back, I wish I had had the wisdom to capture such mundane moments with a camera. Photography was my one art. I earned money selling photos of my valley. I knew what was appealing. Yet, I missed what would become a centerpiece of my life.

When that revelation came, it was not a dramatic epiphany, but rather quiet bemusement. It was a joke.

THE CHAIR

Joke can be another word for "dismissed", as "dismissed" is another word for forgotten.

A joke was how I remember first seeing it through the kitchen window, really seeing it. Even then it was a subtle joke... not a funny grab-the-camera joke, only a reason to pause as pause turns to passing wonder and passing wonder to "what if?" Wouldn't it be something if, under all that paint, there was still enough integrity of wood to both bear a luster and, if reinforced, to even serve its purpose as a chair?

Christmas was two months off. With no money for gifts, I wondered if, with considerable effort, I might give the old chair a new face, well, as much a new face as the chair would allow. Certainly, I had no idea that the joke of that old chair before me was sacred, as ironic humor sometimes is. That chair was the essence of my calling, my door to the kingdom of God. It was to be the parable of hope with which I would relate and come to bless others. Eventually, the chair became a mentor, as it inspired taking the camera into the sacredness of forgotten places. If only I had thought to take just one picture through the kitchen window.

One October day, 1971, with no one watching, I removed the old chair to the garage of Hugh Reed down in the village. In the two months of the chair's renovation, not one mention was made in the family that the old chair was gone from the backyard, a true test of the meaning of forgotten.

In fact, the chair was not pine, as I imagined, but wonderfully formed tiger oak. With each application of paint remover, the old chair emerged from its grunge cocoon, revealing a lace of fine grain. All but a trace of the layers of paint was removed. I kept the traces and, especially, the bottom side of the seat rim where its weathered wood had become gnarled like twisted arthritic hands. The twisted wood and paint residue remain an essential part of its parable of new life. Before one sits in the chair, one tips it back to behold its weathered agony.

For many, it is the hidden warp that makes the chair's embrace sacred and prayerful.

On Christmas morning, the old oak chair made its return. Not given to wrapping such a large present, I covered it with a bed sheet. Such good humor gave "whatever-it-is" heightened curiosity. It was a curiosity turning "ah" to "aha!"

"What a beautiful chair."

Then the truth. Who would have guessed that this was the old chair in the backyard... the old chair, never missed, that now had come home?

"You must be joking."

Suddenly, keepsake, heirloom, centerpiece, the old chair held the moment. It still does more than forty years later.

....

It has now been four years since the project of this book began. Once more I come back to this genesis chapter and, once more, lament the lack of that one photo that shows the chair in its original worn state. So, one last time, I sort through the family's collection of slides and photos, at least two thousand of them, squinting through a magnifying glass at image after image, reducing the many to the few of possibility and then five with a measure of promise.

After two days of sorting, I found a series of slide photos of an employee picnic held in our backyard the summer of 1971. There, in the photos, were a dozen aluminum yard chairs. Popping out among them was the exposed arm of the old oak chair. Another slide captures the arm of the oak chair and a glimpse of the plywood seat. How interesting that in the photo all the other chairs were occupied. The old oak chair was for the latecomer. It was there when all else ran out. Another slide captured the chair at a distance but could not hold up under enlargement.

THE CHAIR

Among the few, there was one of promise. The peeling turquoise legs were evident but not much else. Still, there it was, the old oak chair, a hint of itself, lost in the shuffle, engulfed in shadows, at best a suggestion of a chair. That is as it should be... wonder overlooked, waiting to be discovered. That is where we begin and that is where, in this book, we will return over and over again: a search for the sacred worth of the forgotten.

Life in this one thing.

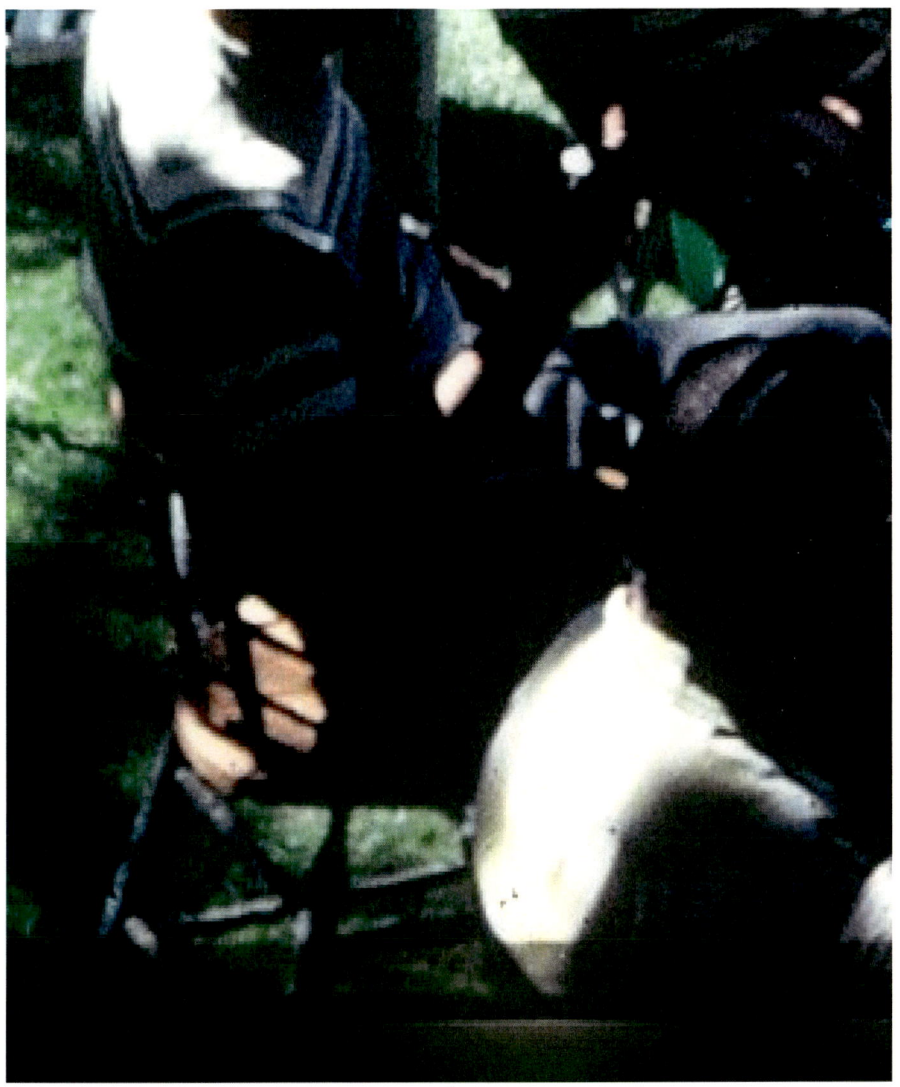

CHAPTER 2
The Parable

I was off to seminary a week after I gave the chair as a Christmas gift. In seminary, I was given the chance to lead worship in a small rural church. What should I preach? It came to me: tell the story of the old oak chair. Preach the chair.

Some clergy spend their lives coming to terms with their first sermon. At least I did. In that first sermon was the mandate for the next 39 years:

There are many lives that are like that old chair,
lives that rot away and never show their real potential.
Too many times it is far easier to discard, dispose or forget
than to cultivate and nourish...
Certainly, the greatest investment,
the greatest accomplishment
is to invest in the accomplishment of someone else.
We must invest our lives in others
before the real dividends in life pay off.
Too many times we do not.
Too many times we actually enable people to rot away—
like the old oak chair.
Parents enraged, who have told their children they were a mistake,
they should never have been born,
or another child forgotten
at the expense of his brother's success.
Older persons, our elders, are often herded out to pasture,
when they still have active, productive talents to offer the world.
There is the one on the job
who becomes the scapegoat for the staff's frustration.
There are those who have paid their debt to society
behind prison walls
but never allowed to become anything more than a con.
We are the generation of Kitty Genevese,
who observe without intervention,
or the crowd watching a person standing on the top of a building,

*threatening to commit suicide
and, from us, comes the sick shout to "JUMP!"
It has become far easier to discard, forget, or worse,
than it is to cultivate and nourish.
The old oak chairs are many.
The carpenters are few.*

In this first sermon, the meaning of the chair evolved from example of renovation to parable of compassion. The sermon then became a beckoning to intervention, to become involved in the lives of others who were like that old oak chair. Finally, the chair stood for redemption. Renovation is not only good; it is beautiful. Such beauty is worth savoring. The old chair became, for me, the central metaphor of being alive in God's love, God as a verb, God as love. The old oak chair was a visual parable of being our brother's and sister's keeper. We were to be the witness of faith, the hands of God, in a time when social indifference, non-involvement, had become a phenomenon coined in such terms as the "Genovese syndrome" or the "bystander effect." The crowd not only ignored the forgotten—the old oak chair withering away—but stood and watched and even relished its demise.

Some asked for a copy of the sermon. I didn't know until later that many of those present in that little church, felt themselves as a community of faith to be like a forgotten old oak chair.

The Baldwin and Monmouth area of Jackson County, Iowa, was known in 1972 as "Welfare City." A representative of the Federal Department of Housing and Urban Development once commented that if he took a picture of Monmouth, Iowa, back to Washington, his office would quickly discern that this town as exemplary of rural poverty. How could that be? Iowa didn't have real rural poverty. Still, there it was.

Midsummer between seminary terms, I received a phone call... would I serve the Baldwin and Monmouth churches? September 10, 1972, I led my first worship service in the Baldwin, then Monmouth churches.

Sunday night until Friday afternoon was given to school. The weekends were given to my student churches. There was a parsonage to live in that had not had occupants for some time.

Each weekend I spread out my sleeping bag on the empty floor. I went to sleep to the sounds of mice crawling in the walls. I awakened some mornings to mice scurrying around my sleeping bag. One night, I burst awake, startled from sleep by a cat fight directly below me in the crawl space. Such intrigue warranted an early priority for a bed and mousetraps.

Such were the distractions from a larger picture of the people I had come to love, my people, not just the church people, but the people beyond the church. Beyond the church festered deep wounds of castaway chairs. With them, the work of hope began. `

Sometimes the work of hope stretched novice ministerial abilities. Shortly into actual ministry, I was approached by a family who felt threatened by a drifter uncle. Off medications, he was hearing voices from outer space. They brought him to me because they were concerned for their children and were afraid to turn him in to the authorities. Since I lived alone in this big parsonage with no furniture, they felt I could give him a corner on the floor and, perhaps, some spiritual guidance.

I called a doctor who asked if this delusional man was a threat. Well, on a scale of one to ten, he was close to eleven. He did not match anyone described in my pastoral counseling textbooks.

"Are you willing to sign to have him committed?" the doctor asked. Well, if the family was afraid to sign papers, I certainly should have reservations. I did not know what to do. Why was the doctor putting the responsibility back on me? The seminary textbook did say, "Know your limitations." The textbook did not tell me what to do when the medical authorities said, "Good luck."

So, I went across the street to my church study and called my church superior. He was seasoned. He took it from there. Through his guidance, other family members were contacted and could be there in a day to decide what to do. Until then, the nephew would take his uncle to a motel and stay with him, so as not to disturb the rest of the family. I, in turn, was to stay in my study with the door locked until they left my parsonage. Thank God for mentoring elders. There is more to tending old oak chairs, people chairs, than removing old paint and applying new varnish.

Green-behind-the-ears, I was the only clergy they had. If not fully prepared, I was fully there. People in need were coming out of the woodwork.

So many who were hurting were young. Once I left for a vacation break. No sooner had I driven away than a young man arrived at my door having taken every pill in the medicine cabinet. He sat on my step waiting and waiting. Fortunately, someone saw him and cared enough to listen and sought other help. More than once, my home was a sanctuary of last resort to youth.

The issue of people on the edge was cause of many good long talks with another elder pastor in the town of Maquoketa. As I told him of situation after situation, he released my anxiety by turning each episode into humor, dark humor, but in its own way, a healing humor.

"What am I supposed to do?"

And he would laugh some more. The only advice he gave me was that whatever seminary might teach me of ministry nothing was going to turn me into a shepherding pastor more than Baldwin and Monmouth. Baldwin and Monmouth might be my old oak chair seeking loving resurrection, but it was also, in return, the hot seat of consternation.

Once, upon arriving home from talking with this elder pastor, the phone rang. At the other end was a faint voice.

"Help."

"Tell me what is happening," I replied with a soft whispered concern.

"Help."

"Are you okay? Is there anyone with you?"

"Help."

"I want to help, but you must help me by telling why you are calling."

"Help."

Then he couldn't hold it anymore and he broke out in uproarious laughter. It was my sick-humored, mentoring elder whom I talked to, savoring every jerking of my chain.

It really was funny. Sort of.

·······

I graduated into ministry more from Baldwin and Monmouth than I did from seminary. Still, the time came to graduate from seminary and Baldwin and Monmouth was a student appointment. A student was all it could afford.

Maybe so, but the work wasn't finished at those churches.

"Yes it is," said my superiors. "You are having a good experience where you are, but both of these are small churches who do not even pay their fair share of the running of the larger church. You have a promising future and it's important that you bring this ministry to a close and assume a pastorate that can afford you and will nurture you on to better things."

As I explain the realities to the leaders of the Baldwin and Monmouth churches, there was a ponderous silence. Finally they said, "Would you stay if we came up with a full-time salary?"

That was not up to me. It was a decision for the higher-ups. So the churches called a meeting with my superior.

"He is not just a pastor to those in the church. He has become a pastor to both communities and there isn't any other resident pastor in the area. We've become churches that matter. We're coming alive and we do not want to lose that."

On paper such a request was a joke. Church authorities were ready to call them on it. "If you can come up with the funds for a full time pastor AND pay all financial obligations to the larger church for this year AND pay all your BACK obligations to the larger church for last year... We will consider it."

Those in authority were sure what the churches' response would be. The authorities were wrong. The Baldwin and Monmouth churches took the challenge. Small as they were, they were determined to keep the momentum of new life going.

When all was said and done, the larger church looked favorably upon such determined spirit. They made an exception. This student pastorate was to become full-time work.

With such approval began a most determined, grueling financial campaign. There were multiple church dinners, a walk-a-thon, even Friday evening gatherings for Reuben Sandwiches, because I could make Reuben Sandwiches.

Notable among these efforts was an exceptional church dinner of morel mushrooms and noodles. In the 1970s, the morel mushrooms of May popped in abundance along the Maquoketa River. Still, it is one thing to find a mess of mushrooms for a family feast. It is another thing to find enough mushrooms for a church dinner. News was spreading fast of this extraordinary offering.

We needed all the mushroom hunters we could find who were willing to scour the woods. In this need came forward a most remarkable man, a quiet, modest man. I remember that he was not literate and, yet, he would stand with dignity, holding the hymnal in tribute as others sang. What he did not have in formal education was more than made up for in his wisdom of the woods. Answering the call for morel mushrooms, he walked miles along the river producing a large 30-gallon bag of mushrooms.

All were amazed and in that amazement was yet another facet of revealing in the wood the fine grain of the old chair. Sometimes, what is most sublime emerges from the hidden corners and the pinewood back legs. It was noted—after this well attended church dinner of morel mushrooms—that the plates returned to the kitchen as clean as anyone had ever seen.

·······

Two small churches could sustain such commitment only by constant monitoring and planning. For a 26-year-old pastor in his first parish, such a fine-tuned operation was a constant concern. I was in over my head. Even more was the growing need, not only to care for persons individually, but to bring them together. They needed to become a collective voice. They needed resources that could nurture them beyond immediate crisis after crisis after crisis. Baldwin and Monmouth were taking a personal toll.

I had gone home to Colorado for some much needed rest. There, in my parents' home, was the old oak chair, defining everything I was living for and needed a break from. After a week, I caught the plane back to Cedar Rapids and made the drive back to Monmouth. There, in the distance, amidst the rolling hills, were the homes of my people. As I pondered being back home, my hands on the steering wheel began to shake. My body was talking to me. It could not sustain such stress. This would be an issue I would face throughout my ministry.

We needed supporting help. The Baldwin and Monmouth churches applied for a grant, asking for funding to support a full-time outreach worker. Two small rural churches, already stretched beyond their limits to pay for a full time pastor, would be willing to raise an additional $1,600 as their fair share, if the larger church would provide the extra $4,000 of what was needed for a church outreach worker. That was a chunk of change in 1974 dollars for two tiny hard-pressed congregations.

Emphasis 72-76 was a mission program that provided a two-year grant. Tiny Baldwin and Monmouth now had a full-time pastor and a full-time "Family Life Development Coordinator." That is how Sheila Kelly came into the picture, and in the whirlwind of her work, the "Miracle in Monmouth" became a story for the front page of the *Maquoketa Community Press*. "Welfare City Myth is Target," read the headlines of January 14, 1975. The front page spilled over into other pages full of pictures and testimonies to the effectiveness of Sheila's efforts and vision.

Sheila took over an empty former roller rink space in Monmouth that had been given to the church. Here was Sheila's office, the classroom for GED classes, a used clothing store, a well-baby clinic, and hot meals for senior citizens three days a week. In the wake of Sheila's work for individuals and groups emerged the Businessmen's Association of Baldwin and Monmouth. Once competing towns were now working together, determined to remove junked cars from the towns and the demolition of derelict buildings.

Community spirit was like an oak chair whose time had come. I smiled to myself as Sheila put into words for the newspaper what she was personally experiencing. "Relating to a small community, *areas that seem to have been forgotten,* has made me realize there is something here which should be preserved."

An old oak chair, indeed.

The local newspaper caught the attention of the regional newspaper, the *Quad City Times* of Davenport, Iowa. The bold front-page headlines of the *Quad City Times* of February 23, 1975 read, "**Young Pastor Brings New Spirit To Small Towns**."

Annamae Staggs, of Monmouth, was quoted in the *Times* as saying that, for her, all of this concern for one another gave "a warmth of security." Randall Edwards, the mayor of Baldwin, Iowa, mentioned that some of what was happening was hard to put into words. It was under the surface. Still, he commented, "Community spirit is tangible. Before, nobody ever bothered to get it going. Now there is a feeling we can get it done."

In June of 1975, I left Baldwin and Monmouth. I hold the memory of flowers along the street as I left. The commitment of the Businessmen's Association to renovation had put planters of flowers around the park. I think they were marigolds. It didn't matter. The beautiful potted flowers were Easter lilies, if only by another name, the finishing touch to the renovation of an old oak chair.

CHAPTER 3
Hari-Kuyo

Five years passed. In those years, I served two different church settings. Both new appointments began with "The Story of the Old Oak Chair." Both new churches in turn seasoned that sermon. Continued graduate work in pastoral counseling refined sensitivities to the forgotten... but only to a point.

The year 1980 brought appointment to the churches of Dow City and Dunlap, Iowa. Once again I gave voice to the truth of my chair. This time, however, the chair spoke back. It challenged me. The chair challenged my honesty. I didn't really embrace all people who were like old chairs, just some. There were some people, old people, I avoided like the plague. These aged people, these often "discarded chairs of society" were the people in nursing homes and other care facilities.

Oh, I did my part. Like every other pastor or priest, I showed up. But it was a ministry of secret dread. I took my monthly rotation among other clergy leading the makeshift worship service in the television room. It was a chore. That chore was summarized in the opening pages of the book I wrote *What Do You Say?* Written ten years later, the words of *What Do You Say?* are now excavated into this story. *What Do You Say?* chronicles the journey from dread to discovery and finally to the transformation, not of the chair but the carpenter.

The Secret Dread

What do you say?
Really.
What do you say?

You open your Bible at the makeshift pulpit before 20 or 30 sets of eyes. You are not sure if some even comprehend where they are let alone who you are. Some eyes are dull, tranquilized, while others dart here and there like nervous tiny birds. Still others placidly wait in acceptance. You wonder how long they have been waiting in those chairs. Chairs are more than furniture here. Chairs seem to be the symbol of the place, symbols of waiting—waiting for what? Waiting to wait some more. No, be honest, waiting to die. Chairs of waiting. When you go you leave behind an empty chair... for a day, before someone else falls in line to wait.

"Lord, what a dismal place." As you say that under your breath, you ask yourself again, "What do you say?" How do you enter this world of empty existence, a world of bingo for bananas, hourly strolls to the lobby, and the endlessly blaring television? Is it any wonder that many older people fight nursing homes as though they were worse than death? "Shoot me. Put me out of my misery, but don't put me in one of those 'hell holes'." They mean it. They dread nursing homes more than death. Nursing homes are no way to conclude one's life. Living isn't living when all the colors have been washed from existence. What is existence gazing out institutional windows to sprawling institutional lawns, or sharing institutional food with those who have become childish and rude in their feebleness?

"Don't send me here to be forgotten and then doped up to endure nothingness in the stench of those who have lost control of their bodily functions. Don't send me here where my life's savings are gone in a year or two, leaving me with no sense of worth in any manner —a spiritual, emotional, fiscal ward of the state. Don't leave me."

Such are the words that fill your mind as you face the eyes that face you. The eyes of those who gave in, resigned to the fact that life must go on even if it has no reason. Again the echo captures your attention. "What do you say?"

One thing is for sure—whatever you say is work, duty. As a pastor, I state it bluntly: speaking of hope is the hardest of ministries to those whose life's beginnings are over.

How ironic that after these years of ministry to the forgotten that the most daunting challenge of "ministerial refinishing" would be in the helplessness of the very old? I feared them, for there was nothing I could do for them. All of these old oak chairs could not play out my truth of renewal. They just sat there looking back until it finally came to me that it was not they, but I, that was in need of "refinishing." It was I that was the old oak chair.

Awakening

It came to me in 1981 at a funeral for a woman that lived to the age of 102. My words of final tribute honored a life that reached back to just after the Civil War. Through her I touched a time of a distant, determining moment in our nation's history. This woman had moved west as a child in a covered wagon and lived to see a human walk on the moon.

Imagine Alvin Toffler is right, that more change occurred during the century of this woman's life than all prior centuries of human history combined. Even if that is only partly true, it is a truth that I touched, if only in her eulogy. Still, that is just the point. I was there to pronounce her benediction from what her daughters told me. I did not bother to ask her to tell her story. She was one of those I avoided. Look what I missed.

This epiphany was followed by the discovery of a box of letters, which were left by my aunt after her death. They chronicled my family's sojourn through the harsh realities of the Great Depression. I did not simply read the letters; I stepped through them, living the moments that were penned on tablet paper by my grandmother. How I now wished I could have asked her about those letters when she was alive.

Between the funeral for this aged parishioner and the letters of my grandmother, something clicked. Suddenly, I wanted to touch as much of the living past as I could. I wanted to listen, selfishly listen. I wanted to step through the cold pages of my history books like Alice through her looking glass. I wanted to reach through, as far as I could, to those who would tell me of a well-lived journey. I wanted to hear of days far beyond my reach, yet still rippling life—life that was *mine* to have for the listening, life given to meaning, energy, and the focus to my own calling as a storyteller.

I felt compelled to become, for a while, a story listener. I decided I would go to the nursing home seeking those souls who would help me feel and absorb the wave of creation from which I was born and upon which I lived my routines. It was as if I was seeking some additional blessing to my ordination. I would not go with pity in my eyes and speak, condescendingly, of the weather. No, I would go with passion to listen. I would go to the nursing home seeking to be ministered to by these frail people who seemingly had nothing in life to live for.

What do you say to people in care facilities, to shut-ins, to any person who, by consensus, reached the point of being old?

Nothing.
If you really care about them,
you go to listen,
you go to be blessed.

How quickly 'awful' transformed to 'awesome,' the chairs of waiting were about to become chairs of couldn't wait. These "empty lives of meaningless existence" were now a hoped-for wellspring of wonder and wisdom.

The forgotten had something to say.

Hari-Kuyo

February 8th is the annual Shinto Japanese celebration of Hari-Kuyo, the honoring of broken and worn out sewing needles. It is, in a larger sense, a reverence for all broken and worn out tools whose "souls still live in us." When I heard of Hari-Kuyo, I was carried back to the lives of those discarded, worn out and broken sewing needles we place in care facilities. Such reverence for me became not annual but a constant observance, and reverence became not passive respect but an indulgent feast of a dynamic, pulsing past.

I could not get enough. "Tell me... remember for me... what was it like?" I asked. I journeyed with these aged elders, my living looking glass to the past. They carried me to a time before automobiles, electricity, and even the final years of the Wild West. These were not vacant occupants of waiting chairs. These chairs pulsed with life.

Her name was Winnie, one of the many who formed my Thursday circle. Her story was only one of several shared that day. An hour and a half later it was my turn to share with the local newspaper editor, "You can't believe what I just heard!"

Winnie was now in her late eighties as she shared the early years of her life reaching back before the sinking of the Titanic, back when, as a young girl in Kansas, she and her siblings bore the tragic death of their mother. As I was to learn, it was not uncommon for a widower father to go out seeking a new spouse on the most practical terms and practical arrangements at a time when some women truly went west as mail order brides.

Winnie in her own words:

"Mom had died. Dad had all of us kids and couldn't cope. He needed a wife and that is what he set out to find. He put all of us kids in custody of an orphanage with a promise to return as soon as he could.

"I was put on a floor with other girls my age, in the keeping of a matron whose discipline was as dreadful as it was effective. If you did anything wrong, she would dunk your head in a bucket of water until you fought desperately for air. I hated her. The place was a nightmare.

"Well, Dad did come back, and we children became a family again with our new mother. One day Dad took us to the fair and amidst the crowd I spotted her, the witch from the orphanage. I became so upset, so angry, I began screaming, pointing at her, telling my father of her terrible acts.

"My sudden commotion drew the attention of everyone, including a politician giving an open air speech. Making the most of the interruption, he had me brought to him. He tried to appease me before the crowd by offering me a little white bear. I told him I wanted to ride on the merry-go-round. I should have settled for the bear. The politician was Teddy Roosevelt."

I sat amazed, living such a magnificent distant moment of history through the aged eyes of once a little girl. I was amazed at Winnie. I was amazed at my whole group. Here were those I once perceived as glassy-eyed stares waiting for the next pill. Here were those waiting to die. I was wrong. We all are wrong. It is we who have glassy eyes. What wastes away in nursing homes, in the homes of shut-ins, and on widows' row of our churches, is our own blessing... the energy, meaning and healing of half of human history, slipping through our fingers.

Eventually, the energy of the Thursday morning group began to call attention to itself, especially on the day that one of my group—confined to a wheelchair—offered to teach me a dance of the 1930s called "The Lame Duck." She in her wheelchair, and I, crouching beside her, began to dance, flapping our arms like a lame duck. The rest of the group joined in, clapping and laughing and stomping to the rhythm of our gyrations. Then the door opened as the nursing staff peered in to see what in the world was going on. The peering-in didn't stop there. The Thursday morning group became more and more a model of ministry *WITH* our elders.

In 1983, I was selected as Iowa Clergy of the Year by the Iowa Health Care Association for this special ministry at the Dunlap Care Center. That was followed by a multi-page pictorial article in the Sunday magazine of the *Omaha World Herald*. Eventually came the publishing of the book *What Do You Say?*

Such was the outcome of facing what I did not want to face. What was first loathed was now one of the chair's greatest gifts. I am glad that the underside of the chair was left unfinished that Christmas season of 1971, leaving a patina of aged layered paint and the witness of the warping and cracking of weathered wood. The chair was not just my story of renovation. It had its own story, its own secrets, just like my old folks who dwelled in the land of the forgotten: the spell of Hari-Kuyo, the reverence for worn-out needles.

James A. Campbell

The weathered underside of the old oak chair

CHAPTER 4
Estrangement

Space was a premium when my parents moved into a residence center. They gave the old oak chair to me. In May of 1990, the old oak chair joined the rest of our belongings as it was stuffed in a shipping container bound for Alaska. Six weeks later, the old oak chair—an object lesson for the first sermon of every ministry—now found new voice in the woods of Alaska.

How far we had come from Iowa. It was a wonder to think that from our new home to the North Pole, there were no fences, only wilderness. Within a quarter-mile of our home were 250 sled dogs groomed for the great Iditarod race. Here we were embraced in the deep night by the dance of the northern lights. Here, for sustained periods, the temperature dropped to forty below zero as we tended the fire of our wood burning stove. Here we would make do with protein from road-kill moose.

Some locals questioned whether we had the resolve to make it. There were times when we wondered the same. Still, we did make it, and, more than endure, we came to thrive in this special place among extraordinary people. Though most who settled in Willow, Alaska, had enough financial security for a comfortable life, many others came to the woods to live off the land. They lived, or tried to live, in anything from a tent to a pickup camper.

One late November night, at thirty-five below zero, we received word that a family ten miles up the road was out of wood. I borrowed a pickup, loaded it with wood and with my son, David, hunted until we found these folks. The couple had four small children. They were making-do in a twenty-four foot trailer with a make-shift wood-burning stove, cutting down and burning the trees around them. Someone had borrowed their chain saw and had not returned it.

The father mentioned, as we unloaded the wood, that they were from central California and had never seen more than six inches of snow and had never been in sub-zero weather before. Then the wife added, "My husband said it won't get any worse than this."

I was caught between compassion and a stare of disbelief. One did not take Alaska's extremes of land and weather casually. The wilderness was unforgiving to people who didn't fit in somewhere else, people who came to Alaska like discarded old oak chairs.

On another occasion, I was called to tend to a family with two small children. They had hitchhiked from Florida to Seattle. Somehow, they had managed airplane tickets to Anchorage and then hitchhiked out as far as Willow. They had no money, no food. A parishioner put them up in an empty mobile home until they could get their bearings.

A visiting church official was with me when I got the call of this family in need. I invited the church official to go along for the experience. When we met the family, they were sitting on their duffle bags in the empty front room.

As I went down my checklist of their needs the official from Kansas asked them, "How did you to choose to live in Willow?"

"That is as far as our ride would take us, so this will be our home."

"You hitchhiked from Florida with two small children, then flew in a plane, and then hitchhiked here and have nothing to live on?"

"This is where God has led us and God will provide."

As I continued, asking questions of their circumstance, the Kansas official looked on in disbelief. It became evident that both children were suffering from ear infections and needed immediate assistance. All of us loaded into my car to make our way to the doctor. On the way, the father inquired if there had been any recent sightings of UFOs.

"No," I answered. "I did hear of a man who was driving north in a fog. He said a strange light followed him, but he wasn't for sure."

When we reached the doctor, I asked how his day had gone.

"Well," he said, "they brought in a fellow who was out of touch. He was confused. He was running down a sled dog trail claiming he was being chased by a dragon."

Then he paused, "Still... he said it was an old dragon."

We returned the family to their lodging. I took the church official to Wasilla, thirty miles away, to make his connecting ride to Anchorage. As we drove he was silent until, out of nowhere, he exclaimed, "This place is NUTS."

"Well, personally," I responded, "I think of it as... character."

"Well, it certainly has characters."

Yes, this was Baldwin and Monmouth, Iowa, on steroids. This is where Charles Dickens would be writing if he were alive today. The Willow I came to know was home for some who did not fit in elsewhere. Willow, Alaska, bore people of raw vulnerabilities. Some Willow folk had convoluted logic extended from often wrenched stories. These were my people. In fact, in time, they would come to be addressed to me as "Your People." They were people who had reason to wonder and hope in the parable of the old oak chair. It was the beginning of my ministry all over again.

But not really.

One comes to Alaska on Alaska's terms, and though the "Story of The Old Oak Chair" was my first sermon in Alaska, it was not a truth that rang nearly so clear as the truth, the parable, that was waiting for me in the Alaska woods... the parable of diamond willow.

....

One can find diamond willow in the lower forty-eight states but, as an art medium, it belongs to Alaska. It is in Alaska that diamond willow is not only found in such abundance, but, also, produces particularly dramatic variations at the center of the stem: red to brown hues and twists of growth that gnarl in sublime sculpture.

There are thirty-seven varieties of willow bushes. Of the thirty-seven, six are prone to produce the coveted twisted wonder of diamond willow. A true token of Alaska is a well-crafted diamond willow walking stick.

So, what is the point? What does diamond willow have to do with the parable of the old oak chair?

There are differing opinions as to whether diamond willow is formed from the extreme cold of the Alaska winter or if it is formed from a disease of the plant. Perhaps it is both. Whatever the cause, it prompts a stress, a perceived torture of the wood. An otherwise brownish-gray, nondescript bush bears an inner resemblance to deep twisted red inflammation. Yet, take the colorful heart of inner wood and sculpt the flow of the strain of the tormented pulp and, first, will arise a sensuous perfume in the sanding dust. Then, with this fragrance, comes the first hint of the elegant, wondrous blend of color and form from the wood itself. A comparison might be the swirl of color and form of red western desert canyon walls that have been scoured by eons of wind and flash floods.

So again, what is the point? The old oak chair was the story of another place, another wood, that was crafted and finished, a wood that was made to appeal and invite. In time, what was beautiful and useful was lost to neglect and decay and then, in discovery, was restored and redeemed. That is the parable I brought to Alaska. What I found in Alaska, in diamond willow, was the parable of a wood that never had its crafted moment. From the beginning, it endured season after season straining against the outer elements and its own inner torment. It was so outwardly plain it didn't blend into the woodwork, it was the woodwork: a single bush among a million lost in the vast landscape of the wilderness. Diamond willow was not made for the antique enthusiast's eye of *Antiques Roadshow*, but for the knowing, discerning artist who sees the promise of incredible beauty that has never been revealed before.

Many people I cared for in the woods of Alaska could understand the old oak chair. They identified and hungered, however, for the truth, the hope of diamond willow. Like diamond willow, many people who never really fit into standards of beauty and acceptability, who never liked the idea of being "crafted" in the first place, might here, in this distant land, find the company of those who would see beauty even in a hard-lived, perhaps twisted and even inner-tormented life.

I came with oak and discovered willow. Willow was both the name of the community I was called to serve and the Alaskan parable in the redemption of its sometimes tormented but exquisite wood. In Willow, I found so many beautiful, wonderful people, if seen on their own terms and in their own wonder, the zanier the better. In Willow, Alaska, one found an abundance of diamond willow people.

Once, I was talking with a church official in a restaurant in Juneau. The person asked, "Do you like it out there in Willow? ...I mean, really like it?"

"Yes," I said, "I love it. Why do people keep asking me that?"

"Because they think you're nuts."

Well, okay. "Nuts" is a fun place to be, a free place to be. More important, I was home. For the moment, I had put aside my old oak chair to refine what was beautiful in the overlooked. I had become a diamond willow man and a diamond willow pastor.

．．．．．．．

When I went "outside," the term given for leaving Alaska to go to the lower forty-eight states, I would share the meaning of our transforming work in Alaska by showing the ordinary appearance of a piece of diamond willow as you would find it in the woods. Then I showed a piece of finished diamond willow. Such transformation was the gospel for the far north. That was what we were about.

The most striking piece of diamond willow I worked was for the Willow church. A wonderful, tall piece of diamond willow was found by Keith Odden near Fairbanks. I took it and let it form itself into a cross. I talked to it as my hands let it release itself. When it was finished, the diamond willow cross was mesmerizing. Its tortured beauty was crowned at the top by what seems to be a fist trying to open. That cross spoke volumes, not only to the holy story it represented, but the people of Willow, so many of whom found this church to be a port in the storm.

....

Attending the needs of those in forgotten corners of the woods became ever more demanding. Willow was to be one-fourth time employment. Another fourth-time was to go to writing. That never happened. The more we lived in Willow, the more it became evident that its needs were all-consuming. My office became more than heaps of "stuff." It was a glorious and total mess. The mess extended from the desktop to horizontal filing on the floor and into the chairs and pouring out into the fellowship hall.

There. There, under a pile of books and assorted papers, was the old oak chair.

There. Clean off the books and papers and pull the old oak chair out into fellowship hall for additional seating at the conference table.

There. Pull up the old oak chair and put your feet on it to rest them from caring for a community of diamond willow needs.

So, if the old chair had lost the force of its meaning, why bring it up? Because sometimes what is sacred to us comes and goes in seasons, and that season of estrangement becomes part of the story. Sometimes, our affinity to whom and what reminds us of who we are, fades away. That can be a part of the journey; a season of estrangement can set the stage for rediscovery, even incredible rediscovery.

That was about to happen in the most wonderful life-giving way. The chair that had become an accessory to my mess was about to come back into my life with a new purpose and force of its own.

CHAPTER 5
Sanctuary

For thirteen years, the chair dwelled in the shadow of the Alaska truth of diamond willow. The old chair finally found a new voice in a program called "Giving Voice." "Giving Voice" was an opportunity for Native elders from around Alaska and across spiritual lines to come together for three days of prayer, reflection, mutual blessing, visioning and shared service, especially to Native youth in the Anchorage and Nome communities. All of these reasons to be together suggested only a vague agenda. The gatherings were free flowing. Above all, the gatherings commenced in prayer: intense prayer. They were prayers expressing yearning for acceptance, healing and hope. All of the struggles of this vast, demanding land, all of the pain of the risks that had taken their toll, all of the worry for children and grandchildren, came pouring into these moments, as profound in silence as they were in uttered reverence for God and one another.

It was in the gift of sharing such prayer that it came to me. Get the chair. I went to my office and brought the old oak chair into the fireside room of Turnagain Church. The table was removed and the old oak chair was placed in front of the fireplace. There I told the Native elders the story of the old oak chair. When I was finished, I invited one who had just unburdened her soul to sit in it as the rest of us surrounded her with a laying on of hands.

The grace of God flowed in that moment, in us and through us. As a river it flowed. In that moment, the old oak chair became the blessing chair. After prayers for one were said, a second asked to be embraced in the chair and a third and a fourth. No longer was the chair simply a parable for what new life can be. The chair had now

THE CHAIR

become sanctuary, a sacred place to go for prayer, for blessing.

The next day the chair occupied the center of our room, representing the holiness of what we had shared the night before. As we continued in reflection, word came to me from the pastor of a church whose congregation was using our facilities, that he was about to perform a wedding.

"Well, when the wedding is over, have the bride and groom come and join the elders in our gathering and we will pray for their marriage.

And, that is what happened. The bride sat in the old oak chair and the groom stood behind her as the elders of "Giving Voice" gathered round and blessed them into their

The elders with the chair at "Giving Voice."

new life. What the night before had held the cares of the world was now a focus for joyous celebration.

The next day the elders were scheduled to go to Alaska Children's Service, which is a treatment center for troubled youth. Seeing the possibilities, the elders asked that the old oak chair might go along, that its story, parable and presence might be an inspiration.

From that moment on, the chair became "the blessing chair," a movable, single-space sanctuary, indoor or out, formal or informal, for a moment alone or a gathering. The chair was living parable, a holy embrace.

Word spread about the chair and the gathering of Native elders. A year later, I had just concluded leading worship, when a young woman came to me needing to talk. As our conversation ended, she asked if I would pray for her. As I bowed my head, the young woman asked, "Where's the chair? I would like to sit in the old chair."

She made me smile. I went to my office and brought the chair to the front of the church, and there, we lifted her concerns to God. It dawned on me, as we finished, how the old oak chair had taken on a life of its own. For thirteen years, the chair had become incidental, indeed, replaced by the more dramatic Alaskan parable of diamond willow. Now, a gift from my Native Alaskan Elders at the gathering of "Giving Voice," the chair not only returned as a vital instrument of ministry, but had also transformed from parable to a prayer sanctuary.

....

In June of 2009, our nineteen years of ministry in Alaska came to an end. Once more we became Iowans, with our residence in the eastern Iowa town of Belle Plaine. Once more was preached the same first sermon that now was 37 years old. This time, however, the old chair was not just a visual sermon parable. From the very beginning at Belle Plaine, the old oak chair was the blessing chair. Within weeks of our arrival, it became "sanctuary" to a young woman beginning in ministry, as the church surrounded her in prayer. From then, it appeared frequently enough in Belle Plaine worship that its presence was anticipated. It was used to bless a young woman going in mission to the earthquake-ravaged people of Haiti. It became an insistent part of another woman's pilgrimage into the ministry. "My last Sunday in Belle Plaine, I want to sit in the blessing chair."

One would think that would be the end of the journey, but the journey was just beginning.

CHAPTER 6
Iconic

Before the wedding of our son David, I invited him to sit in the old oak chair and then blessed him into his new life. The next summer was David's twin brother Doug's wedding at Lakeside, Ohio. The packed car heading to Ohio included the old oak chair among the luggage.

Once again, it became a chair of blessing and, later, graced a wedding photograph.

Then came the epiphany. Waiting for the reception, I walked to a grassy expanse that opened to a view of Lake Erie. It was a nice setting. Still, what would happen if the old chair was centered in the grass, pointing out to the lake?

Adding the old chair completely transformed the view. Why?

My cousin, Dr. Allan Campbell, of Peoria, Illinois, was taking pictures of the wedding. I asked him to photograph the old chair by the lake. This photo haunted me for weeks to come. Why does an empty chair so completely alter this setting? Would it do the same to any other setting? Suppose, instead of the chair, I put a pot or vase? They, too, changed the character of the photo, but not anything like an empty chair... and, it had to be empty. An occupied chair did not have the same effect.

Photo courtesy of Allan C. Campbell, M.D.

There was something about an empty old chair that forced a special wonder.

After all these years, I was at a wedding by the lake, seeing the chair, once more, for the first time. The chair was not only parable and sanctuary, it also iconic, in so much as iconic means anything that helps us see a larger beauty or truth.

Out of the blue came the inspiration for a road trip... road trip to where? It had to be to 'a land forgotten.' I would take the chair to the empty lands in the center of what once was the Dust Bowl.

As a youth, nothing was harder to endure than traveling through eastern Colorado. This was especially so if travel was in the summer back when cars had no air-conditioning. Our annual pilgrimage to Iowa to see family always meant the hot dry air isolating each of us into our own silence as we counted the miles across the endless monotony of Colorado's eastern plains. By late youth, I had pegged this desolate, boring landscape as "Grapes of Wrath National Park." Here, once, great winds of dirt scoured the earth in monster clouds that rivaled any vision of horror movie hell. My Sunday School teacher had lost two children to dust pneumonia near La Junta, Colorado. It was torture in those dust bowl days. I didn't need convincing.

Now, the same land that I abhorred was beckoning. The older I get the more I yearn for solitary places, forgotten places. The vast open land that was a dread of my youth becomes now enticing, even sacred.

....

Preparing for the adventure required training my mind to see with a "chair's eye." With the help of a friend, Don Prichard, we spent the afternoon posing the chair atop an amazing tree stump, then in a cemetery with a tree that had a lone branch reaching out across the graves. Finally, we came upon just the right spot on a country road.

THE CHAIR

There it was. There was the spell of the empty chair, even if I could not say exactly why.

．．．．．．．

The journey of the chair "to the land forgotten" began in Fort Collins, Colorado. That is where I met friend and photographer Vernon J. "Jim" LaBau. Jim flew down to Colorado from Alaska just to share this screwball adventure. Not everyone is inclined to follow a chair through the Oklahoma panhandle.

I needed Jim's technical skill in photography and, more than once, it was Jim who would see the "chair moment." I also needed Jim's eye for detail. As a forester, Jim was given to recording the specifics. Jim was the scout for snakes. Most important, Jim was keeper of the story. As we traveled, Jim read excerpts of Timothy Egan's *The Worst Hard Time*. This book became our mentor. The book was our guide as we made our way, wondering where the chair wanted to go next through the lands of the Dust Bowl.

Before the journey, I pressed the fact that I had no plan for travel save general directions. The journey needed to be totally spontaneous. We relied heavily on whim. One road was so remote in southeast Colorado that the GPS had no record there was a road before us.

As a matter of record, our journey to the land of the Dust Bowl went southeast from Fort Collins to dwell among the plains and hills of southeastern Colorado. From there we journeyed to the region of Boise City, Oklahoma. Here was at the very heart of the Dust Bowl. Pushing then south we searched the vistas of Dalhart, Texas, before moving back into Oklahoma. Finally, we returned through Texas to New Mexico. In New Mexico, we followed the eastern edge of the state to Roswell before making a diagonal meandering to Albuquerque where Jim LaBau caught the plane for home.

Such a journey with a chair's eye was as inspiring as it was exhausting. We didn't want to miss a chair moment. Still, we didn't know what the next chair moment was until we came upon it. It can be disconcerting, not knowing where you are, looking for an unknown destination. Still, this attune-ness to the unfolding landscape, making twists and turns without regard for time or immediate destination, created an excitement, an anticipation to travel that no planned itinerary could ever provide.

Everyone should have the ecstasy of traveling aimlessly with a chair's eye. It took one week to make this wonderful adventure and four years to understand it.

"LET THE JOURNEY BEGIN"

Jim LaBau and Jim Campbell

CHAPTER 7
Of Loss and Whimsy

The most common response to the meaning of the empty chair is loss. It is the grief of the empty chair at the table. It is the art of empty chairs at the memorial for the victims of the Murrah Federal Building explosion in Oklahoma City. The empty chair was the poignant understatement at Oslo in 2010. The presentation of the Nobel Peace Prize to Poet Laureate Liu Xiaobo was marked with an empty chair. Liu Xiaobo was locked up in a Chinese jail.

An empty chair is emptiness. Dr. Allan Campbell, pondering the empty chair that remains in tribute to all who died in the most horrific Civil War battle of Antietam writes, "The empty chair is a person lost, by whatever means, a loss." This is the chair's message at our point of departure. We left Fort Collins heading into "the big emptiness" of eastern Colorado to the crossroads of the settlement of Last Chance. Last Chance was "Empty Chairville." We began to play with the sign and the chair, seeking each to define the other. Finally, I happened upon the chair tumbling into the sign. It was amazing how the image was at once tragic and comic, tragic-comedy like a stumbling clown.

An empty chair is a symbol of loss in the right context. Context is everything. Take the chair out of a somber circumstance and the resulting incongruity turns it into whimsy, even a parody on loss. "Falling out of one's chair" is what you make of it at Last Chance, Colorado.

·······

As we traveled further southeast toward Springfield, Colorado, Jim LaBau read as mentioned, excerpts from

THE CHAIR

the work *The Worst Hard Times* by Timothy Egan. As we drove, we imagined, through Egan's dramatic words, the towering rolling tsunamis of dust consuming again and again this land and its people. One year there were seventy dust storms. The energy of the clouds was so intense that barbed wire fencing turned red like the heating elements of an electric stove. The dust swirled and gathered into what were called "Black Blizzards." They suffocated many to death in a new disease called "dust pneumonia." Many left to become unwanted "Okies." Others stayed to face what more and more were calling the end of the world. Woody Guthrie captured the moment in his song, "So Long It's Been Good To Know Ya." Multiple verses were added as each additional facet of dust bowl endurance begged to turn tragedy into comedy.

We crossed into the Oklahoma Panhandle. Jim asked me to stop at the Cimarron River. He held the book up. "There it is. There's the river." In the worst of times, the ground was so devastated that nothing grew between horizons. Layers of dust upon dust created a monotony of brown. People drove for miles to what was left of this river just to see something green. Others would hold to the hope of a lilac bush that survived against the side of the house. For others, it was a tree or a house plant. The promise of something, anything, green, became sacrament against the consuming relentless force of rolling dust upon dust.

Down the road, rising from the long-since healed landscape, was the earth aglow in yellow daisies. We placed the old chair in the embrace of this color burst. Here, once more, was tragic comedy. The chair casually accentuates the whimsy of spring, new life dancing in full bloom, reaching to a welcoming vast sky. At the same time, the chair's emptiness amidst the flowers is a memorial to those who lived this very world, waiting for the sky to turn, through the most intense of ecological disasters.

The whole point of tragic comedy is not to choose, as I tried to do at Last Chance. Tragic comedy is to hold both extremes at the same time, letting each help define the other, while creating a larger vision of struggle, endurance, acceptance and hope.

....

The scene now changes to a jumble: random, discarded, strewn refuse often found along some forgotten dead-end road. The photo has no real focus, no

THE CHAIR

symmetry. Nothing fits. It trips over itself. The photo is irritating, like a tramp clown suit of stripes and plaids.

Look closer at the chair, the clown's sad eyes. The chair faces away from the old plow to a plain of grass that has reclaimed the land, a forgiveness. Clowns often blend whimsy and loss and forgiveness, naming hurts, weaknesses, disappointments, and at the same time, making them sublime. In this "clowning" of the chair, we hear the echo of pioneer Caroline Henderson in her work, *Letters From The Dustbowl*. "We dream of the faint gurgling sound of dry soil sucking in the grateful moisture of the early or later rains; of the fresh green of sprouting wheat or barley, the reddish bronze of springing rye. But we awaken to another day of wind and dust and hopes deferred..." (pp 146-47).

The chair's clown eyes look away as it unites the plow and a broken water pump, remnant icons, dust bowl relics... the plow, ill-used, and the well gone dry, the brokenness of bad choices.

....

In stage drama, there is sometimes used what is called a "reveal chair." It is a chair on a swivel that is used to emphasize a surprise twist in the plot. A character is talking to someone facing away, when suddenly the reveal chair spins to disclose that the one in the chair is not the person we were led to believe was sitting there, or we discover, when the chair is spun, that the person in the chair is dead.

On our journey, we discovered, quite by accident, our own "reveal chair." At a small roadside park there was a perfect rock to capture the essence of the "chairperson." A chairperson is one who has "taken the chair" and, thus, "chairs the meeting" and, by implication, is in charge of "the floor." In academia, the chair indicates knowledge and authority at the university... a chair, perhaps in physics, is given in memory of one remembered for their excellence or at least their fine donation to the university

THE CHAIR

coffers. The newly appointed professor bears the honor of first assuming the chair and then holding it.

I placed the chair on a proud protruding rock. There it was, the elevated chair, the "taking of authority chair" rising to the occasion on the podium. It was the noble academic chair of pure imagination.

But then, aha! ...the reveal chair, the swivel chair turns (well, we walk around it) and VOILA! There is the true face of the chairperson. He or she has been at the meeting so long as to turn to stone with blank, staring eyes, still open, but whose snoring mouth betrays.

Still, look again. If the point of the chair on the rock is simply the joke of a swivel chair, a play on those who take authority, then we miss the truth of the moment. Note the wear on the near side of the rock in the first picture. It is nothing compared to the deep, deep carving of the wind from the west. In spite of the bluff behind it, the rock's exposure to the west wind left an old tired man with deep, sad, expressionless eyes, ravaged skin, gasping for breath. The east side of the rock is smooth, majestic hope. The east is where the settlers came from, where their dreams came from, dreams that called them to take and take some more, this virgin land of the "reveal chair."

Still, that is what it is, a swivel chair, a reveal chair, a chair that weighs how every truth, every hope, every taking, can have a dark side. "Beware of taking and how you take," says the old man of the rock. "Don't feed the wind more earth than what it already takes." That's what it says, this Mount Rushmore of the Dust Bowl.

THE CHAIR

The "taking chair" bears witness to the old man in the rock. He was there when they came for the taking. They didn't listen. They just took from the earth.

The old man is still speaking.

....

It is a subtle but profound difference in one who "takes the chair" and the casual invitation to "grab a chair" or "pull up a chair." One is raised authority. The other is welcomed community.

The older folk whom I served in Iowa remember "Kansas passing over." The dust from the west forced people inside. Hundreds of miles to the east the skies grew brown in Iowa. In Iowa, they were putting towels to the windows to keep Kansas from breaking and entering. There was drought in Iowa, especially in that summer of 1936. They knew hard times; not Oklahoma hard times, but they knew hard times.

In previously discussed work at care centers, the listening to the stories of my elders often returned again and again to the Great Depression. Many of the Iowa old folks relished those demanding times. "We didn't have much, but we had each other." For all else that was lacking, there was always, "Pull up a chair." The Depression was pull up a chair time.

This had special meaning on Saturday afternoon when people went to town. One could pass the time on the porch of a store sharing the week's news and watching the parade of folk that came in to shop.

"Pull up a chair." Maybe that was a key difference between Depression times in Iowa and Depression times in the Oklahoma and Texas Panhandles. Many people lost their farms in Iowa. They went under. They had it hard, but not like Oklahoma hard, not like the Okies loading up to leave. One third of the population was gone by the mid-30s and the rest were wondering how long until their turn.

Caroline Henderson, in her letters, spoke of the eerie loneliness on a Saturday when folks were supposed to come together. Instead, she remembered driving the state highway during these hard times. She mentions maybe meeting one car while passing empty house after empty house. In Oklahoma, the very fabric of community was ripped apart as people pulled up a chair and sang, "So long, it's been good to know ya."

Again and again, community bond was forged out of more than want. There was the additional prevailing fear of the next dust "roller," forcing children to run home from school. They huddled in their living rooms as the black blizzards tore the last vestige of paint from the house. When the dust storms hit, the static electricity was so palpable and intense that it shocked persons to the floor. People, desperately needing to be together, kept their distance.

In the end, the spirit of community that held all the country together during the Depression was there in the

THE CHAIR

center of the Dust Bowl. It was just different. When it was over, Iowa would look back in reverence, "We had nothing, but we had everything, because we had each other."

Western Oklahoma didn't look back. It was too painful. For them, there was nothing but the whistle of the wind and the last ones left standing in a game of musical chairs. There comes a point where even the clown stands still and waits for the wind to finish.

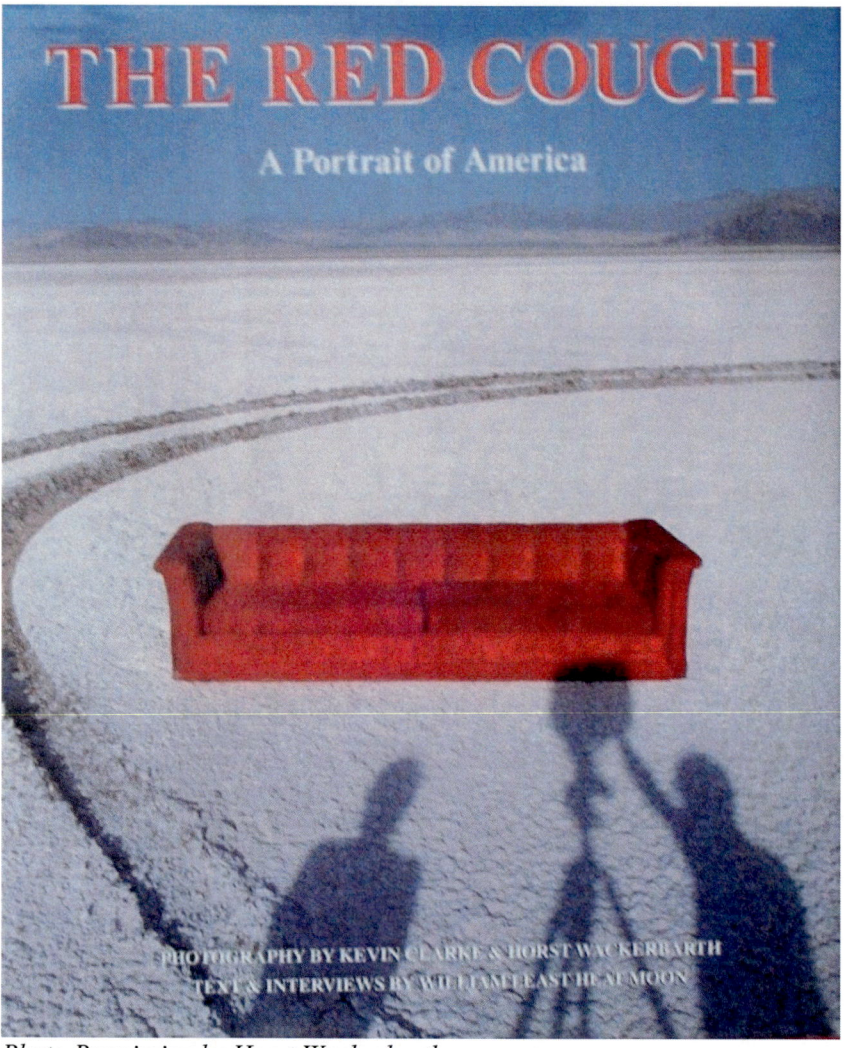

Photo Permission by Horst Wackerbarth

CHAPTER 8
Unique

It was the winter after our sojourn to the Dust Bowl that I received an Internet link to a newspaper in Pittsburgh. The web site was a photo essay of chairs after a snowstorm. Until then, I had not given thought that others might ponder the truths of chair-ness. In fact, I was not alone at all. My sister Jane called most excited. She had attended an estate sale and came across a copy of the book, *The Red Couch,* with photos by Kevin Clark and Horst Wackerbarth and text by William Least Heat Moon. The work was a tour de force portrait of America, transporting a red couch to remarkable settings around the nation capturing the faces and stories of who we are as a people, sitting on a couch.

Receiving the book from my sister was demoralizing. Traveling with a piece of furniture to force wonder and truth was MY IDEA. My epiphany was a unique epiphany. My road trip was... "different" and I relished that difference. I had pushed Robert Frost's "A Road Less Traveled" to new dimensions. Jackson Pollack had his breakthrough with drips of paint; this was my breakthrough with "chair-ness." I traveled the open road with inspired confidence, going to nowhere as no one had before.

With *The Red Couch*, I felt like a doctoral student finishing a dissertation only to find someone had written it all. The introduction to *The Red Couch* detailed the account of Russell Maltz discovering the couch, then seeing its artistic potential to sift first humor, then meaning and form from what otherwise was absurd incongruity. He then refined the vision until he made his own journey. Each situation demanded constant rearranging and fine adjustment until the couch said,

"This is it. This is where I need to be in this setting." One needed to know the couch's persona. They needed to know how to talk to their furniture. Well, of course they did! I knew that. It just never occurred to me that others talk to furniture.

Then I noticed an old friend, well, an old book. It was Kenneth Burke's essays entitled, *Perspectives by Incongruity*. Half a century before, Burke addressed the issue of forcing incongruity to transcend the boundaries and blinders of stale certainties. Guess what he used to illustrate his point? A table chair! Take a table chair and put it in a totally different context.

As I read it, I laughed out loud. I wonder if Burke pushed his truth until he personally knew his chair and listened intently to where she wanted to be placed to make the right statement.

I was standing in a crowd, a crowd of chair people. How much of a crowd? I found a website to "The League of the Empty Chair." These were empty chair enthusiasts

THE CHAIR

AP Photo/J. Scott Applewhite

who pondered in repeated sessions, "Why are people fascinated by empty chairs?" Yahoo has a photo site of nothing but images of empty chairs. Then I discovered Robert Crawford's poem, "The Empty Chair." He reflects on the meaning of the empty chair by the seaside... so much for my grand discovery at our seaside wedding. Then again, Yahoo not only has a photo site of empty chairs but a separate photo site of dozens of empty chairs by the seaside.

One person from the "The League of the Empty Chair" nailed it. "The empty chair is a universal icon." Never was that so driven home as at the Republican National Convention of 2012 where Clint Eastwood talked to an empty chair.

For days the airways were filled with empty chair jokes, including a viral Internet revision of Mount Rushmore with the four presidents and a chiseled likeness of an empty chair.

I was walking not a well-traveled trail but a multi-lane icon autobahn. So the choice... I could either succumb to the crowd or see these chair (and sofa) aficionados as fellow pilgrims of Chair-dom. Even with such resignation, I was not prepared for what was to follow. It is one thing to share the same general ballpark with others. It is unsettling to discover a person who is a mirror image of your own epiphany.

His name is Donal Moloney, an accomplished photographer who lives in Ireland. First, I found the website, www.donalmoloney/storyofchair, then other on-line tributes to Moloney's work, finally making e-mail contact. Donal Moloney is not only a man with a camera; he is also a man with a chair, a chair that journeys, just like mine. Even more, Moloney's chair is personal. He calls it, "Chair."

Moloney writes, "It seems like Chair has taken over a permanent seat in the back of my car. He ignites people's curiosity every time I frame him in front of the camera and briefly becomes a minor celebrity. I usually tell them

Photo Permission Donal Moloney

the story and before I know it, I'm using their mobile phone to take a shot of them sitting on Chair."

Moloney's story bears a striking resemblance to my own. It is a story described in the publication *Totally Dublin*:

> *"We have witnessed Chair alone at the beach, unexpectedly in the ghetto, surrounded by less than friendly characters, in nature, in the kitchen, on public transport. There is no prescribed pattern, he is wandering through life, ambling along, finding himself, luckily or unluckily, wherever he arrives. The likeness between Chair's story and the story of* **Chair** *is uncanny. It is a classic case of life imitating art or vice versa. Neither have a real plan, both are closing their eyes and feeling the way forward allowing the inevitable to happen*

> *while simultaneously enticing what has the possibility of passing by unnoticed. There are layers of life lessons and understanding embedded into The Story of Chair."*

This was amazing. My touring in the middle of nowhere with a chair was so absurd, but not so absurd that someone else a third of a world away wouldn't be compelled to do the same.

One wonders, how many others around the world were making journeys in the spell of empty chairs? Such sparks the imagination to a potential comedy or horror movie: *Night of the Chair People*. Or perhaps some cruise line might offer a cruise for chair people. For those too lazy to travel with their chair perhaps one could download an online virtual tour of a recliner.

Then again, for all that might be out there or could happen, I needed to make the most of what I already had. I sifted back through the wonders of fellow chair pilgrims until I found a mentor, not of empty chairs, but empty roads. His name was William Least Heat Moon, the one who wrote the text for *The Red Couch*.

CHAPTER 9
Dust Brown Roads

William Least Heat Moon is best known for his acclaimed award-winning work, *Blue Highways*. Robert Penn Warren said *Blue Highways* was "a masterpiece... Least Heat Moon has a genius for finding people who have not even found themselves." These folk were back roads folks, people of the blue roads on the road map. Main roads were red; secondary or back roads were blue.

On our road trip we started out on blue roads that on the map turned into even more remote black roads, then gray roads and finally a few that were dotted lines. One road, as earlier mentioned, wasn't even on the map or recognized by GPS. Our chair led us to the end of the road. When one runs out of roads one runs out of people. Unlike Least Heat Moon, who went to remote byways looking for conversation, we made do trying to make sense out of the silence of small weathered cultural remnants protruding through the buffalo grass.

Who knows, perhaps this protruding rusted piece of farm machinery was witness to that time of the Dust Bowl. With no Dust Bowl travel brochures, we were left to fend for ourselves as we imagined what once was. So it was that we found a lone fallen, sun-bleached tree along a gray highway, stretching between a black highway and a dotted line somewhere in the middle of our need to remember.

The tree itself was a wonder. We began to play with that wonder. We hung the chair from of a branch, placed it beside the trunk, placed it in the cleft of the branches.

Trying this and that for five minutes, we finally had our epiphany. Instead of finding the right way to picture the chair with the tree, we had the tree embrace the chair. The two together formed a wondrous invitation to behold the vastness of the prairie.

Behold

"Fallen Tree" was a monument. It gave focus to this once great drama. Timothy Egan summarized the find of such a tree. "Occasionally, a visitor comes upon a row of elms or cottonwoods, sturdy and twisted from the wind. It can be a puzzling sight, a mystery, like finding a sailor's note in a bottle on an empty beach" (p.310).

Here, at this tree, this "bottle on an empty beach," our chair's eye peers into the bright sun of Palm Sunday morning, 1935, looking to the north, waiting, as this very sky manifests into Black Sunday with towering clouds of angry wind and dust pouring over the earth. Three Hundred Thousand tons of earth, the sum of the dirt dug from the Panama Canal, came pouring over that horizon in that one afternoon.

Then it dawned on me, the road on the map beside this tree should be colored dust brown. There should be a sign along the road that reads "Point of Interest." But there is no sign by Fallen Tree. One stops because the chair says, "stop." If one stops long enough to imagine the drama of the dust bowl, it begins to feel like standing before a great battlefield. In a sense, that is what it was: a horrific war with nature.

....

We continued along our Dust Bowl highway reading Egan's book and imagining those years of incredible trial. Suddenly, we were approached by… a bicycle race.

One wonders what the cyclers thought as they pressed on in the searing heat, passing an old chair in the middle of the road.

What is that about?

Indeed.

I gave the cycling photo by Jim LaBau to artist Anne Whitfield. I asked her to blend the cycling photo with perhaps the most iconic, poignant photo of the Dust Bowl, a photo by Arthur Rothstein, taken in April of 1936 in Cimarron County, Oklahoma. From Anne's effort came a time warp unity of a dust brown road, our time imposed on the time of the Dust Bowl.

The photo strains to reach the time of storms. Caroline Henderson, in *Letters From The Dust Bowl*, writes, "We are in the worst of the dust storm area where William Vaughn Moody's expression, 'Dust to eat' is not merely a figure of speech, as he intended, but the phrasing of a bitter reality, increasing in seriousness each passing day. Any attempt to suggest the violent discomfort of these storms is likely to be in vain except to those who have already experienced them" (p. 140).

The chair directs us to the windowless house standing naked but for tarpaper shreds. Who is this man as pitiful remnants of fence posts joke of the boundaries of his home? Where is his vehicle, his escape? Is there a wife

THE CHAIR

Rothstein Photo/Library of Congress

waiting inside or is it just him and the children? April 14th was Palm Sunday: the beginning of the walk to Easter. What did Easter hope mean this year as every hope of life is buried and buried again in dust? A crop is not going to happen. Nothing is going to happen. Why is he there? How does he feel knowing that a stranger in the distance is taking his picture? A picture of what? A picture of a man who won't give in to, "So long, it's been good to know ya."

What then of the children? Is either yet alive? How was it for them to live the terror of the storms? What of this struggle did they carry with them? Did they move on, choosing not to look back?

The more we try to capture a moment, hold the moment, define the moment, the more we realize how much we do not know. We realize how much we cannot behold. Still, even with what little we do know, wonder crosses over into reverence. The chair is not simply beholding the drama before it, but hallowing it.

The same day I was writing these thoughts, I happened through the main lobby area of the regional library. In a large glassed-in display case was an open bound volume of the local newspaper. As fortune would have it, the issue of the paper on display was the front page of April 21, 1936, the same month as the Arthur Rothstein photo.

On the front page were two large photos of a family seeking escape from the Dust Bowl, stopped at the Colorado-New Mexico border atop Raton Pass by Colorado State Troopers. The large bold headlines read: STATE TROOPERS HALT PARASITE PARADE.

Is that what the Okies were, parasites? I returned home to study further the Rothstein photo, all the more drawn to the chair's focus of those entrapped in the earth's revenge of people's poor choices.

Then: the interruption. Riding on the edge of gathering, advancing clouds of dust are cyclists lost in the race of the dirt brown highway. They are of this moment. They are us, coming towards us, focused on the race and its destination. They are riding in the moment of a past forgotten, oblivious to what once was. The old chair is simply a curiosity in the way.

One travels the red to blue to black to gray to imaginary dust brown highways seeking vistas to imagine and remember all those in the old photographs of the Dust Bowl. At the same time we see ourselves. That is us lost in the race, in all of our races of the world, going faster and faster. The immediate race and gratification of the moment tempts our focus to straight ahead. How easy it is to miss the whispers of the wind as it sifts dust and judgment over highways and destinations.

CHAPTER 10
The Enigma

This chapter begins and ends with the same picture, but it's not the same picture at the end, not at all. Its simplicity is deceiving. Its simplicity is haunting. Its simplicity is its ultimate truth.

First impressions suggest balance, diversity in unity, a wholeness of form. It is the chair at the gate of an abandoned house that is lost in a vastness of grass ascending to the hills on the horizon. It is a pastoral scene. When it was shown to others, some commented on its colors, its composition. One mentioned how, as an Old West relic, this rock-faced abandoned house was an iconic cowboy home. "Then again," someone else notes, "imagine the scene in winter. Imagine this house in blizzard-strength gales with snow drifts halfway up its windows."

Such were obvious truths. They did not touch the core of what made this picture compelling. What was it? This picture is a parable that wouldn't tell its truth. For months I stared at this riddle of the chair and the house and went nowhere.

In western spirituality, parables, on the surface, bear a truth that is simple, obvious. Then again, the simplest parables often have deeper meaning. Sometimes a parable becomes a riddle, a riddle that leads deeper into ever increasing enlightenment.

My picture of the chair at the gate of the old ranch house became a riddle of questions within questions. I needed a mentor who knew the way of the chair and abandoned hut. My mentor's name was Gaston Bachelard.

Gaston Bachelard lived in my study, on my shelf, in a book called *The Poetics of Space.* Through his printed words, Bachelard took me on a walk deep into the meaning of the house... every house that is truly a home. To understand the meaning of the old house in the picture one needed to know its secret... the secret of the daydream. Houses were made in which to daydream.

Bachelard was a most esteemed professor. He held the chair of the Philosophy of Science at Sorbonne University in Paris. He was a

Gaston Bachelard

master of reason and the processes of critical reasoning in both philosophy and science.

Bachelard's colleague, Etienne Gilson, writing in the preface to *The Poetics of Space,* noted, "...the future of Bachelard's career was easy to foretell. Having specialized, as they say, in the philosophy of science, he was likely to write a dozen more books on the same subject. But things were not to be that way."

No, indeed. Throwing caution to the wind, Bachelard proclaimed that for both science and philosophy to be complete, each needed imagination, not just practical imagination, but the power, the authority of... the daydream.

Bachelard's colleagues said, "WHAT?" Actually, colleague Etienne Gilson exclaimed, "What are they going to say? Who, they? Well, we, all of us, the colleagues." The faculty was stunned. Why do philosophy and science need daydreaming? Their response echoed for me back to grade school.

I do not remember a single grade school teacher that blessed daydreaming. Daydreaming meant you were not focused, you were not paying attention, you were not thinking. Daydreaming was laziness and could be a reason for discipline. It was certainly an indication that you were not learning. They gave no grades for daydreaming. I wonder what my teachers would have thought to hear Bachelard, this master of science and philosophy, say that without daydreaming, education, even to the far reaches of science and philosophy, was incomplete.

During the week, we traveled with our chair; we turned here and there on a whim looking with "a chair's eye." Caught in the spell of the chair's eye, were we daydreaming? Is that what the chair caused us to do? I wanted to think so.

Even so, what does that have to do with the chair sitting before the old house?

The riddle—the walk with Bachelard—continued.

It is necessary, says Bachelard, for scientists and philosophers to become poets, for it is the poet whose realm is the daydream. So Bachelard, a philosopher of science, writes not the "Analysis of Space" but the *Poetics of Space* and does so with a poet's voice, uniting awareness and imagination in a celebration of essential daydreaming. Daydreaming is how we think beyond our box of reason if we are to get beyond the limitations of reason alone.

How do scientists or philosophers give themselves to daydreaming? One might begin by discovering the energies of our dwelling, the imaginative power of home. It is our house—our most intimate habitat—that begets the daydream. Bachelard writes:

> *"If I were asked to name the chief benefit of the house, I should say: the house shelters daydreaming, the house protects the dreamer, the house allows one to dream in peace. Thought and experience are not the only things that sanction human values. The values that belong to daydreaming mark humanity to its depths... Now my aim is clear: I must show that the house is one of the greatest powers of integration for the thoughts, memories and dreams of mankind"* (p.6 Beacon Press edition).

With that, Bachelard explores the effect on imagination of nooks and crannies, each room and its doors and furnishings, each window with its light and shadowed nuance, the hallway, the attic, the cellar and the thresholds that invite one into and between the rooms of the house. In all of it are the corners, the sacredness of corners, in our corner of the world. *The Poetics of Space* is a tour de force of how home is the sanctuary of the dreamer. Some call Bachelard's book "The Bible of Architecture."

So, the questioning continues. Are there dwellings given more to imagination, to dreaming, than others? Is there a true poet's home? Yes, responds Bachelard, there is, above all… the hut, the simple hermit's hut, standing alone in the vastness. The hut is the elegant simplicity of the most intimate space, furnished by light's drama and the daydream.

How great is the desire to see the place where a great writer wrote or a great artist painted. Occasionally, one is given the chance to sit at their desk and look out their window and recite what was dreamed, what was birthed, in those walls. Writes Bachelard, "The old house, for those who know how to listen, is a sort of geometry of echoes." That is particularly true of a poet's hut.

There it was, my chair at the gate of, what for me, needed to be a hermit's hut, a dream place, a poet's house in the vastness of a forgotten land. In a sense, this picture of the chair is a self-portrait of yearning, naming, dwelling in the sacredness of dream space. This one picture is the summary, the riddle, the koan's journey of the old oak chair as it came to dwell in this great vastness. If there was any destination, conclusion, to our travels, it was here.

James A. Campbell

The Old Oak Chair at the Threshold of the Hut

CHAPTER 11
While Waiting For the Story

In the last chapter, mention was made of how long it took to realize the truth of the chair at the gateway to the hut. Waiting was a norm. Through the years of writing this book, the words did not always come easily. Some days the words flowed faster than I could write them, sometimes not. Sometimes they did not flow at all. This was due to the self-challenge of taking a week's journey with the chair and then searching out the meaning, the truths, of dozens of photographs from that week. The wisdom of the journey revealed itself while endlessly staring at pictures I knew had something to say but were so slow to speak or would not speak at all. Staring at pictures, waiting for their truth, takes its toll. The "chair's eye" that was directing where to go next in the panhandle of Oklahoma was now giving me "the evil eye." Over months and months one can get chaired out, one can have too much chair. One can find themselves in the hut yelling, "I gave you life, now speak to me, you Pinocchio hunk of wood!"

Talking to a stubborn chair that will not speak creates a whole new venue for writer's block. It pushes the envelope of creative boredom. Boredom from "the block" is necessary to daydreaming. There are the fallow times, necessary seasons of "imaginary drought" to confront, while dreaming in the hut. Sometimes one just stares out the window and draws a blank. That is life. Knowing how to take boredom in stride, to wait well, is a virtue to all those who live for imagination's gifts. Prolonged staring at a chair and its pictures, asking for its secrets is a whole different kind of boredom. Boredom sometimes forces lateral thinking—thinking to the side—allowing our distractions in boredom to open doors we would not have otherwise tried.

·······

Woven throughout the book is a thread of comic truths. The book began in comic irony, then whimsy, and then explored comic tragedy. Now in the distraction of chair staring is the door to comic relief. The right frame of

...And the chair replied, "Actually, once I was a tree."

mind turns every serious chair photo of this journey into a cartoon. All it needs is the right caption.

I could have made a cartoon book called *Travels With My Chair*. Several photos that are especially given to comic captions are set aside for future projects. The chair's "eye" had a propensity for mischief and the ridiculous during the trip. One can only contemplate the Dust Bowl so long without comic relief.

Still, is that it… amusement? Where does comic relief lead? The more comic the chair becomes, the more personal it becomes. In humor, the chair becomes human. In the caption above, the chair actually talks. It actually does become a kind of Pinocchio.

When we befriend the inanimate we often project our most basic human needs. Similarities come to mind. They took blankets and began to waltz with them in the Australian outback until the blankets became partners and finally they gave them a name, Matilda. In the movie *Castaway*, Chuck Noland (Tom Hanks), stranded in isolation on a desert island, starts throwing things in rage including a Wilson brand volleyball. Later, he ponders his bloodied handprint on the ball. He turns it into a face and then begins to talk and relate to the ball named "Wilson."

Making human the blanket, the ball, and the chair with a flower, creates an immediate comic response. Hopefully, comic relief turns to empathy. We begin to feel for what we have created. Such compassion sometimes becomes sublime, beautiful. What is beautiful draws us further in. We become "in touch" and caught in the energies of our own creation.

It happens sometimes when one is writing a story. The characters of a story become so alive they eventually seem to write the story. It is comic, really. Sometimes it feels as if what we are creating is bringing us along for the ride, just to set the story on the page.

If we are lucky in those moments, what we have brought to life makes us in turn that much more alive to what is around us. At least that is how it felt traveling with the old oak chair. I created the story scenario of "following the chair" on this journey. I created the notion of a "chair's eye." I chose to go to "No Man's Land." It was a comedy set up. Then the seriousness of the story of the Dust Bowl set in. Traveling the dust brown highways became tragic comedy. We needed the chair to make us laugh. We need comic relief. The comic relief, of simple, beautiful amusement, made us all the more "in touch" with this sacred earth and its story.

That's what the beauty of comic relief did to us. It made us all the more one with the earth. We stopped at totally forgettable places and touched the earth. Each stop was beautiful. It was beautiful because the insane comedy of following a chair gave us cause to laugh, to wonder, to feel and touch and touch and touch. Touch creates intimacy and simplicity. Touch turns prairie grass into elegance.

The following photo is one reason we found to pull over. Since no one else stopped, there was no "condemned" sign, no "DO NOT ENTER" on the wall. It was incongruence, comic, to put the chair beside the entrance. Still when I did, there it was. Just the right cast of light on the arm of the chair led the eye into the recesses of the worn walls, then to the wonderful verticals of framing and the soft hazed light on the road and fields beyond.

What did the picture mean? That did not always matter. Not everything is story with some deeper truth to explore. Everything on this trip had comic potential. In turn, often the comic moment yielded to what was lovely to see and lovely to the touch. It was beautiful and that in itself was reason enough to even make the trip, let alone to live a life.

Such is what I finally discovered when the chair refused to speak.

THE CHAIR

CHAPTER 12
Going Home

THE CHAIR

After the great road trip, the old oak chair made its way back to Belle Plaine, Iowa. Another year passed and then came the most glorious finale to thirty-nine years of ministry. The people of Christ Church prepared a most thoughtful, jubilant celebration that led me into retirement. That service, so rich in memories that still fill my thoughts, concluded with one last blessing.

It was my turn to sit in the old oak chair. With wife Maggie beside me, the congregation blessed us into our new life, paying tribute not only to years of service but also to "the blessing chair," which the congregation had come to love.

There was only one problem. When the service was over, we had no room for the chair in our car as we made our way to retirement in Beulah, Colorado, where I grew up and where the old oak chair began its story. Thus, for a year, the old oak chair was in the safe keeping of John and Jeani Brandt. During this year the old chair made new friends.

The following summer, the old oak chair was readied to make its journey home in grand style.

Finally after forty years, we both were home.

Still, what is home?

I have given wonder to my relationship with my chair, how it has become a part of me. It makes me think of the one who made stone soup. Put a stone in a pot of water then start adding what complements the stone: this vegetable and that, a pinch of this herb and some salt. Then add some beans and maybe some beef stock and before you know it you have a pot of real soup. The stone, of course, is really incidental, a catalyst. Then again, if one makes stone soup enough times, I can imagine developing a discriminating, subtle taste for stone. Some may say that it is all in your head. I suppose that is as good a place as any. That's where I keep my chair.

THE CHAIR

POSTSCRIPT

"So, what are you writing about?"
"I'm writing a book about my life with my chair."
"...oh."

This book is, in fact, about an evolving relationship to a chair. It is more than that. This book is about knowing. It is a book about discovering catalysts that can enable us to expand from awareness, to the comic, to the beautiful. It is a knowing that fleshes out the spiritual mandate for justice and empathy, to live for what is healing, joyous, and redemptive. Perhaps one may call it catalytic knowing, the poetics of stone soup.

It may be that the future belongs to those who are given to multiple ways of knowing, multiple ways of discovery, play and assimilation. To such an end is the offering of this book.

Made in the USA
San Bernardino, CA
07 January 2015